Outfox the Fox

Understanding Manipulation

Learn the Hidden Secrets of Power and Influence

Table of Contents

Introduction

Regardless of the type of manipulation you are seeking to understand, outwitting it is going to require awareness and patience. Through the discoveries of Anthropology, we have found that throughout all human history there has always been aggressive behavior to further one's own desires. Seduction, persuasion, influence, exploitation or manipulation, whatever English word you use to describe it, the fact of a matter is that everyone is trying to have control over you for their personal interests either consciously or unconscious. The word manipulation is generally perceived negatively but it is essential to accept manipulation exists or nothing in this book will be of any use. We all use a degree of manipulation throughout our daily lives. Some, however, take it further.

Human interaction is always going to be a tricky thing. Since birth, you have always been taught that you can't possibly find much success in this world unless you know how to play nice with others. Even at a young age, the principles of proper decorum and social conduct are embedded into your system. Think back to your earliest memories. You probably have vague snapshots of your mom or dad teaching you the basics of the alphabet. You probably remember being oriented with names of animals, colors, shapes, and certain objects around the household. But along with that, if you had relatively conventional and responsible parents, you probably remember being taught about manners and a code of conduct. You are taught these things because your parents always want for you to be likeable. They don't want you to end up not having friends when you grow up as a result of social ineptitude. Along with any cognitive or arithmetic skills that are developed in early childhood, you are also essentially taught how to be a social creature. This is because the common belief is that you are always going to need other people in this life to get you to where you want to be. It's just how our society works.

This all stems from the fundamental idea of people in your life serving as assets who can help add value to your existence. If this is the kind of mindset that you have, chances are that you are a generally optimistic and trusting person. However, the truth is that optimistic thinking might not necessarily always translate to real-life situations. As humans, we all try to gain favor of the people around us. Not everyone serves as an equal asset to each other, there will always be people who offer less value to your life than others. That is a safe assumption to make. But also, we are primarily driven by our own selfish desires and intentions. And sometimes, our personal desires don't always merge seamlessly with those of others. As a result, conflict may arise. This is where the nature of human interaction gets even more complicated. In these moments, we might try to engage in some form of conflict resolution.

For the more civilized and well-natured of us, conflict resolution isn't necessarily going to be such a stressful ordeal. Those who are adept at resolving conflict know how to conduct themselves properly and always act in good faith. They show a willingness to engage in civil debate, persuasion, and constructive dialogue to come to some kind of middle ground or understanding. However, not all of us are going to be so willing to take the high road. In fact, a lot of us are going to play dirty to get what we want, it brings out the primal nature of our species, the animal side if you will.

This is exactly where the art of manipulation comes into play. To be perfectly blunt, every one of us has the capacity to be manipulative. In fact, we might have dabbled in manipulate behavior to a certain degree, think back to all the different conflict situations throughout your life that you can remember. While you may not have cruel intensions, there are those of us who take the art of manipulation to a whole new level. And that's what this book is going to be dedicated to: the identification and understanding of these types of people. When it comes to situations where manipulation is involved, it's either you are the predator or you are the prey. Whether you decide to become a predator is your business. You might get a lot of backlash for being manipulative (if you get caught), but you might also have your reasons. But whatever the case may be, no one ever wants to be the prey in this scenario. And the most important thing that you have to do to avoid being the prey is to arm yourself with the knowledge and wisdom that you need to protect yourself from manipulative behavior.

Another side of the word "manipulation" is commonly used describing events in our lives we did not wish for, or supposedly had no conscious control over. People love to casually claim "manipulation" over things to imply they can't be held responsible over things that have happened to them. It can be argued that these types of people even want to be manipulated, as it can seemingly help them evade responsibility, in fact, they are the easiest pray for manipulators. It is crucial to take responsibility in order to spot real manipulation. There are plenty of things you have control over, but there are also things you have absolutely no control over, do not waste your time and efforts on the latter. It may not be easy at times. Accept this fact deeply and you can start to see things as they really are with efficiency.

Based on infinite number of individual factors in your life thus far, you likely have your own prior cognitive biases and beliefs regarding manipulation. This book is not an attempt to state what is right or wrong, good or evil. We are taking a precise, neutral view on a complex and serious topic. It's an attempt to form a deep understanding of manipulation and how to combat it. This book is going to be a contribution to the global dialogue surrounding manipulation. You will discover how manipulation can make an impact on your own personal life. We are also going to look into practical real-life instances on how certain timeless manipulative tactics and philosophies have helped shape the trajectory of human society all throughout history.

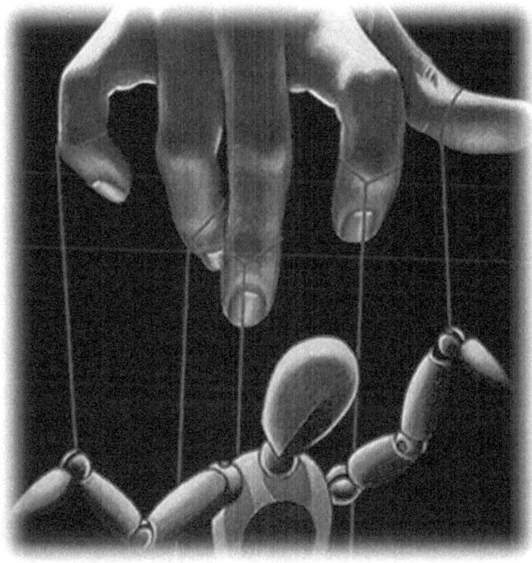

For many of us, the very first thing that comes to mind when "manipulation" is mentioned could be an image of someone pulling the strings on a mass scale like a puppet master. There may be manipulative establishments in our society but in the western world especially, practically everyone is free to choose what they want to do in life. It is also important to consider manipulation in our daily interactions, as those are likely the more immediately applicable cases you can begin to work on. Try to come from a place of autonomy. In a negotiation, debate, or anything that requires influencing others to do what you desire, have no-deal as an option. We often fear of losing things we don't even have yet.

Manipulation in the Modern World

Don't be so naive to think that manipulation doesn't exist in your world. If you truly believe that, chances are that you often find yourself being a victim of others manipulation without even realizing it. Consider this textbook scenario for a moment:

Jessie has plans to do X. Nathan has plans of doing Y. Jessie and Nathan have a cordial relationship with each other. However, they have fundamental differences in the way they are choosing to approach this one scenario in particular. Nathan has tried to convince Jessie that Y would be the better approach here. However, Jessie has shown no signs of budging. In this case, civil debate and persuasion comes into play. This is why Nathan is thinking about employing the following tactics:

1. Nathan will use his charms to try to break down Jessie's emotional fortitude.

2. Nathan will resort to certain hyperboles or exaggerations to make the Y approach more appealing than the X approach.

3. Nathan will make Jessie feel guilty about choosing the X approach.

4. Nathan will divert Jessie's attention to one aspect of the X approach that he knows will make Jessie fearful or apprehensive.

5. Nathan will do something nice for Jessie prior to convincing her that the Y approach is much better so that Jessie will feel more obligated to listen.

6. Nathan will convince Jessie that doing the X approach is going to make her look bad to friends and family.

7. Nathan will threaten Jessie with the termination of their friendship if Jessie chooses to stick with the X approach.

Every one of the tactics listed above can be considered as a form of manipulation. Granted, these are all very simple and digestible manifestations of the art of manipulation. However, you would be mistaken to think that this kind of toxic behavior can't be scaled up. In fact, as you make your way through this book, you will come to discover just how far you can take the art of manipulation as long as you're cunning enough. Manipulation can come in various shapes, names, and sizes. For instance, a lot of people would refer to tactic number 3 as *guilt-tripping*. Tactic number 6 is also commonly referred to as *peer pressure*. Tactic number 7 is something that most of us would identify as *blackmail*. They are all different approaches to manipulation, but they are all consistent in one thing: they seek to fulfill selfish desires at the expense of another person's preferences.

In the modern world of technology and instant gratification, manipulation can strike anywhere and it can come from anyone. When you're a kid who is still living with your parents, you might find yourself being manipulated by them, aside from your delicate childhood where you took in all of the opinions and ideas from your parents and friends, both the good and bad. They tell you that if you don't follow their rules and regulations, you should find a new place to stay. This is a form of blackmail. When you are working, you can also experience manipulation at the office. You might be contemplating leaving your workplace because of the toxic environment. But then, your boss gives you a small raise and additional benefits. After that, they ask you to stay and you feel obligated to do so. This form of manipulation seeks to induce a sense of obligation within the victim to get them to do something that would benefit the manipulator. Again, there are simply countless different ways and magnitudes in which manipulation can manifest itself to boil it down into a simple definition. And it's always important that you are able to keep your basic defenses up just to make sure that you don't fall victim to these common tactics.

Where there are humans, there is opportunity for manipulation. Don't think manipulation is limited to only the physical world. It is very much present online where many are willing to do anything to gain more attention, money and influence. Questioning beliefs is especially a common trick nowadays over the internet in order to bait or attract people into giving them attention, now it is very likely that you have some beliefs that could very much be incorrect in some way and at times you must in fact; *"unlearn what you have learned"*. Being open for change is at utmost importance but the key here is to remain objective and neutral when taking in new ideas or questioning your existing beliefs or biases. With anyone being able to spread information globally, the mixture of information has never been higher. Particularly the online "guru" phenomenon has grown widely over the past few years. Verify your sources on significant matters. Think to yourself what do they benefit from you taking the action they are suggesting. Do they practice what they preach? If you have time to reflect on your own, i.e. the practice of simple meditation *(not to be mistaken with extended spiritual type of meditation forms unless preferred)*, you are likely to remain in a more relaxed and rational state. Such rational, relaxed state of mind is always ideal for overall intellectual decisions.

Infect people with the proper mood, make them feel good about themselves, manipulators want to be perceived as someone pleasurable who everyone wants to spend time with. For instance, would anyone share the dull and ugly parts of their lives in social media? The best manipulators never get caught, it's all about the image they create. Lying blends in strongly with this strategy. Naturally, most of the viral content tends to utilize plenty of manipulative traits.

In the palace nobody ever wanted to be the bearer of bad news even if they had nothing to do with it, knowing the king could have them beheaded for simply being the messenger of troublesome news. Sophisticated manipulators use the surrounding culture and its norms to their advantage. They tend to have a sound understanding on how specific things have more weight in different cultures and for different people. Remember, manipulators, persuaders, seducers, are not self-centered, quite the opposite in fact. They are focused on understanding their target, playing on the victim's ego or subconscious mind. The more subtle manipulators and seducers often develop a specific type of pleasing trait(s) since a young age. Pablo Picasso and Giacomo Casanova, for instance, were rumored to seduce hundreds of women all the while making each of the woman they seduced feel like just they were the special one.

The Problems with Manipulative Behavior

You might be unsold on the idea of another person's manipulative behavior being damaging and dangerous to your life. And that's fine. There are a lot of people out there who have a generally optimistic view of the world. These are the kinds of people whose dispositions are always positive as they always expect the best out of others. You might be someone who wouldn't think it possible for anyone to do substantial harm or damage toward another human being. However, this kind of naivety could put you in a compromising position. This kind of mindset, while noble, can put you out of touch with reality. The truth is that not all people are always going to have others best interests in mind, in fact, it's quite rare.

A lot of the time, an individual's selfish desires are going to be able to overcome their willingness to do good for others. It's just an unfortunate fact that our own selfish desires aren't always going to coincide with the best interests of other people. Ideally, we'd all drop down our individual differences and work together towards the betterment of all everything, see the earth flourish, discover the unknown and advance our resources, knowledge and so. However, in reality we have to deal with our ever so changing, and at times pesky emotions. Taking the time to understand manipulation is just as, if not even more helpful assuming one's intensions truly are righteous in nature.

This is exactly why manipulative behavior persists to be so prevalent in modern society. One might even be able to make the argument that in a globalized world where power is continually becoming decentralized, there is more incentive to take advantage of other peoples' potential to gain a competitive edge. But that's another debate altogether. The point here is that manipulative behavior is toxic, and it has the potential to negatively influence a person's life in a significant manner.

To get straight to the point, the biggest problem with manipulative behavior can be measured by the harm that is inflicted on the targets of this behavior. When done conventionally, manipulation is usually carried out in an aggressive manner. There are many possible intentions that can go behind one's manipulative tendencies. However, it can be generalized in either of these two instances: to directly harm the target of the manipulator or to benefit the manipulator at the expense of the victim.

The negative effects of manipulation are especially evident in romantic relationships when two people have a connection that is more intimate and close-knit in nature. In these cases, it's not rare for subtle and nuanced manipulative behavior to eventually evolve into physical abuse and domination. However, manipulation can also wreak havoc on more public platforms. For instance, manipulative advertising and marketing can lead to consumers making ill-informed buying decisions based on fraudulent claims. In business, there are numerous exploitative contracts that are being made left and right that are built on manipulative tactics. Manipulation is also largely integrated in political systems of the world. With "fake news" and "alternative facts" being hurdled around by people in power, it can be rather easy to sway a voting public to behave a certain way. This kind of manipulative approach to governance can pave the way for tyranny and totalitarianism.

The Other Face of Manipulation

It is a long-held belief that manipulation is harmful and that causing harm to another human being is morally reprehensible. Of course, at face value, it can be very easy to automatically brand all forms of manipulation as bad. However, if you really try to study the art of manipulation, even though its methods are always devious in nature, the intentions are not always to cause direct harm toward another being. In fact, there are some (albeit, very rare) cases when manipulation might actually seek to benefit the target. For instance, take the example of a father who lies to his child about the idea of Santa Claus. He tells his kids that they must always practice kindness, love, and generosity so that Santa will reward them with a nice gift come the holiday season. He also tells them that if they misbehave, Santa will only gift them with a lump of coal.

Obviously, now, as adults, we are able to identify this as a case of manipulation because we know that the idea of Santa Claus is a mere fantasy and folklore. However, if you look at the intentions of the dad in this scenario, he simply wants to make sure that his kids always do good even when no one else is looking. Granted, his paternalistic approach to inducing kindness and generosity in his kids might be manipulative. But his intentions can't necessarily be classified into the category of manipulators who seek to inflict harm on their victims. Even if the parents don't know any better, their possible "manipulative" acts often come from the right place of heart. This is when the art of manipulation seems to fall into a gray area, and people might still debate whether a manipulator's intentions can alter the moral value of the manipulative behavior itself. We all see things based on our own reality and detractors of this kind of "benevolent" or "paternalistic" manipulation structure their argument on the idea of manipulation being a violation of one's autonomy. Thus, revealing the real vagueness around manipulation and making it hard to define in simple dictionary terms suggesting it should rather be viewed as more of an art than a science.

Manipulation as a Violation to a Person's Autonomy

You might have noble intentions when you manipulate a person or you might not. Whatever the case, there is an argument to be had that manipulation is always going to be a morally wrong concept due to the fact that it violates the autonomy of the individual. This is the reasoning that goes behind this train of thought: when you manipulate someone, you are trying to influence that individual's capacity to engage in decision-making. However, how manipulation differentiates itself from rational persuasion and debate is that it does not seek to enlighten or educate someone about an alternative perspective. In that regard, with slight alterations or skews of the facts surrounding an idea, there is a definite interference with the autonomous decision-making capabilities of a human being. Essentially, the choice to make an autonomous decision is undermined by a person who engages in manipulative behavior.

It's important to stress this point because there are plenty of manipulative people out there who excuse their behavior out of a sense of self-righteousness. And whether or not their arguments have merit is totally up to you. But for the purposes of this book, it's important to provide an alternative perspective on the matter just so all bases are covered. Again, gaining a better understanding of manipulation and the nuances around it will equip you with the knowledge that you need to defend yourself from it.

Understanding How to Deal with Manipulation

At the end of the day, you're going to have to deal with a lot of manipulative people in your life. You are going to expose yourself to manipulative behavior in varying forms and degrees. It's a safer bet to be on the dominant side of the human nature and expect this to be a constant in your life no matter who you choose to surround yourself with. That is why you always want to be making it a point to try to understand this kind of behavior and the depths behind it. If left unchecked, manipulation might actually inflict a lot of harm and damage to the lives of so many people. In this book, you will read about how manipulation was used to advance the personal interests of a select few at the expense of the many. You are going to be exposed to the many ways that manipulation can manifest itself and what kind of damage that it can cause to an individual.

If you also happen to subscribe to the idea of manipulation being a violation to a person's autonomy, you would be better equipped to handle paternalistic approaches to deceit and fake news. The best way to arm yourself against manipulative behavior is awareness. Make an effort to understand it better. The most dangerous enemy is the kind that you don't know even exists. This is why knowledge is power. And in this case, knowledge is also protection. It's not only enough to deeply understand manipulative behavior but to also know yourself.

"If you know the enemy and know yourself, you need not fear the result of a hundred battles. If you know yourself but not the enemy, for every victory gained you will also suffer a defeat. If you know neither the enemy nor yourself, you will succumb in every battle."

– Sun Tzu, The Art of War

As you make your way through the chapters that will follow, it's possible that you might gain a better appreciation for the art of manipulation. You might even come to admire the cunningness and the intelligence that goes into being able to control a large group of people in a single instance. There are certain nuances there that certainly warrant some level of admiration, or at the very least, respect. But again, as to whether you will use this knowledge to be a force of good in this world is up to you. The mere point of this publication is to act as an impartial medium offering you deeper insights and a more profound perspective on what manipulation is, what it looks like, how it gains power, and how it can be stopped.

Chapter I: The Ponzi Scheme - A Systematic Guide to Manipulation for Greed

In this chapter, we are going to take a deep look into the famed Ponzi scheme. You might already have some kind of exposure or familiarity with this scheme especially if you have a background in finance. But more than just being a big financial issue, the Ponzi scheme actually carries a large emotional component with it as well. It's an apt case study into the power of manipulation as a tool to fuel and satisfy one man's greed. It touches upon the devious and manipulative tactics of one man that would leave lasting remnants on the face of financial power play, not just in the United States, but on the world.

A Brief History

The year is 1919 in Boston, Massachusetts. Charles Ponzi had received an International Postal Reply Coupon from a friend in Italy. Ponzi had noticed that the coupons were originally purchased in Spain even though they had been initially been sent from Italy. He discovered that this was because the coupons were cheaper to acquire in Spain. The coupons could be used to exchange for local post office stamps in the United States. In fact, given the exchange rate of U.S. and Spanish currency at the time, one would be able to exchange for up to six times more than the usual amount that you would get for a locally-sourced postage stamp. Ponzi saw a very unique value proposition here, and it was then when he put his plans into motion.

Using the Spanish coupons as inspiration, Ponzi devised a massive scheme that involved him taking peoples' investments and converting them into Spanish pesetas to purchase International Postal Reply Coupons. He would then have these coupons sent to the United States to be then used to redeem postage stamps. These stamps could then be sold for dollars at a profit. In theory, Ponzi's plans were foolproof, and they would prove to serve him well for a short time. However, what he and many of his investors didn't anticipate was that the exploitation of these price discrepancies on the international market would correct itself overtime. Therefore, this wasn't a very sustainable business model.

Nevertheless, Ponzi established his company with the sole purpose of exploiting this discrepancy between international postage stamp trades. He called it The Security and Exchange Company. You might have this confused with the Security and Exchange Commission, but the SEC wasn't founded until the 1930s.

Ponzi was quick to get to work in his efforts to pool funds together from as many people as he could. He promised potential investors that they would be guaranteed a 40% return on their investments in the span of just ninety days. Given that interest rates at the time were around five percent per annum, Ponzi's offer was just too good to pass on. Notably a bulk of the people Ponzi approached were composed of the immigrant community of Northern Boston.

It all started with just a few modest investments in the early months of 1920. Ponzi then decided to up the ante by promising a 100 percent return on investment in just the span of ninety days. Obviously, given his very tempting and uniquely packaged value proposition, the cashflow was off the charts. He had six people under his employment who were working around the clock to manage all of the money that was coming in. Ponzi then decided to put all of that cash into a mutual savings bank. To those who are unfamiliar with what a mutual savings bank is, it's much like a credit union wherein depositors buy shares within the bank. Due to his large sums of deposits, Ponzi soon found himself to become the majority shareholder of the bank. He eventually became the president of the financial institution.

Ponzi then found himself to be really busy as he was tasked with handling large amounts of money and acquiring various pieces of real estate. He was definitely living a life of wealth and luxury that most people can only dream of. He got so busy with all of the money that he was handling, and he ended up neglecting the International Postal Reply Coupon scheme that had earned him his money in the first place. All of the profits that his organization was making was only the result of the interest of his bank deposits.

An Investment Too Good to Be True

By mid-1920, the Boston Post had published an article that touched on the implausibility and flaws behind Ponzi's business model. The supply of International Postal Reply coupons just didn't add up to the kind of returns that Ponzi had promised his investors. A lot of investors approached Ponzi with the intention of earning a large amount of cash within a short period of time. And after the piece that the Boston Post had published, plenty of investors were worried. They decided to demand their money back from Ponzi because they wanted to get out immediately. Ponzi then used checks from Hanover Trust Bank, a bank that he had gained control over, to pay these investors off.

In an effort to do some damage control over the Boston Post article, he promised investors that he had another scheme that was in the works. He also had the gall to say that this scheme would produce more money than the postage coupon scheme. Ponzi was able to convince so many people to buy into his new promises that he gained an additional couple hundred thousand dollars' worth of investments.

However, it wasn't just the Boston Post that was being a thorn in Ponzi's side. The District Attorney of Boston at the time directed an order for Ponzi to stop taking in new investments for the Security and Exchange Company. The D.A. claimed that there was a need to audit the company's books. In addition to the D.A. going after Ponzi, another Boston Post article was published. In this new piece, the Post had gathered information from a man who had formerly worked for Ponzi's company. Their source claimed that Ponzi was one million dollars in debt and that Ponzi was depositing funds into his bank that was earning as much as five percent interest in a year instead of focusing on making profits that could yield hundred percent returns in ninety days.

It was also during this time wherein the Post would be able to unearth Ponzi's storied history. He was originally born in Italy, but then was migrated and was raised in Canada. He had dabbled a lot into work that involved him arranging money transfers with Italian immigrants. There were reports of a lot of these remittances never having come to fruition. He also had his share of jail time in Montreal for forging signatures. Once he was released from prison, he had to earn a living through menial jobs such as clerking and washing dishes. It only changed for him in the year

1919, when he had discovered the International Post Reply Coupon discrepancies.

Essentially, the Security and Exchange Company came crumbling down as a result of all the news pieces and audits. He had been estimated to owning around 7 million dollars (equal to roughly $ 200 million today). The Hanover Trust was also closed down by the Massachusetts State Banking Commission. However, Ponzi was quick to realize what was happening and had taken out one million dollars from the bank. He used this money to bet big on the Boston racetrack in an effort to try to keep his company liquid.

Ponzi was arrested and was charged with grand larceny and fraud. He then defended himself by saying that the people in power were only trying to punish him for offering a more level playing field that would allow for the "little guys" to make just as much money as the rich. Ponzi went to prison once more but was released on parole after three years.

The newspaper articles and the audit of Ponzi's Security and Exchange Company destroyed the scheme. The Massachusetts State Banking Commission closed down Hanover Trust, the mutual savings bank Ponzi was president of, but not before Ponzi took about one million dollars to a Boston racetrack to bet on some long shots in hope of winning enough to make his company solvent.

However, even though he was released on parole, Ponzi would find himself at odds with the law once again. He was rearrested for violating his parole. He then decided to jump bail and changed his name. He moved to Florida, where he would later be arrested again for real estate fraud. He had promised a 200 percent return in a span of sixty days to various potential investors. He was able to jump bail once more, but then he was eventually captured and extradited to Massachusetts. He was sent back to prison for another seven year.

Once he was released from prison, he was deported to Italy, where he would struggle to find consistent work until his uneventful death.

Ponzi's Manipulation Tactics

In this case, Ponzi tapped into the very nature of human greed to satisfy his own greed for money. He wanted to live a life of comfort and luxury. However, he knew that he wouldn't be able to do that alone, or didn't want to. This is why he decided to use other people. He manipulated them into thinking that they would all get rich together as long as they jump on board with him. In essence, the greedy Ponzi capitalized on the greed of other people by making exorbitant promises that he had no intentions of keeping.

He knew that many people had shared his desires to become rich. It was all just a matter of devising a scheme that would be able to lure a lot of people like himself into the whole foray. However, financial analysts and experts would tell you that a thorough analysis of Ponzi's business model would actually be easy to say no to. There was just no way that Ponzi would be able to fulfill his promises with the money-making scheme that he had set up. But Ponzi knew that peoples' greed would get the best of them, and he capitalized on that fact. He knew that the sheer desperation to get rich would be enough to entice someone to go against their own better judgment.

It should also be noted that the less knowledge of a topic person has, the easier it is to manipulate them towards what you present. And here's where Ponzi's main targeting came into play. Rather than a person who has mastered a specific skill, find the unsuspecting rookie. Any attempts to manipulate a person who knows the topic inside out, say in this case any economics or financial investment related, are likely to be called out as they can see beyond the fluff and trickery. Manipulative people know giving out simple promises, tips and tricks for free that supposedly act as valuable information for a beginner will gain them people's trust over time where they then can start offering their paid" expertise".

Manipulators often have you rush decisions, creating a sense of urgency on the case. We tend to make poor decisions under pressure and with time on their side you are likely to make a decision without sufficient information. They present something as confined, a special opportunity that just happens to be easily accessible right at the moment, but only for a limited time. Manipulators always want to keep the victim reacting instead of rationally thinking about the situation, and as we know, money is one of the most powerful objects for turning us into emotional, reactive state of mind. Acting in the emotional state naturally requires less effort than thinking something through rationally, which requires great effort and is rather tiring.

The Ponzi scheme was simple, and it's not too hard to see why so many people fell for it. After all, who wouldn't want to get rich quickly? Even though his promises seemed to be too good to be true, Ponzi's charisma and manipulative prowess made him convincing enough for people to actually buy in.

Don't think the times of people falling for Ponzi schemes or scams are over, quite the contrary. To this day, there are plenty of manipulative individuals out there who pattern their scams after the Ponzi scheme. And there is still an alarming number of people who fall for this tactic every day. Only in the very recent history there have been plenty of massive scams where the manipulators managed to utilize human greed with very simple protocols; Bitconnect, Madoff "investment" scandal, Allen Stanford's scheme and so on. Avoiding these types of schemes or scams is rather simple, establish deep, core values you strongly believe in. But it is easier said than done, you must truly stand by these principles. A person who deep down disregards the "get rich quick" mindset is less likely to be lured into any sort of a scheme by even the most cunning of manipulators.

Chapter II: A Napoleon Complex – Mass Manipulation to Amass Power

In this second chapter, we are going to take a look at the life of one of the most prominent figures in world history, Napoleon Bonaparte. With people who aren't really familiar with Napoleon's story, he is known to be one of France's greatest champions when it was just starting to get back on its feet following the French Revolution. However, to those who studied him extensively, they would know that Napoleon was amongst the true masters in the realms of manipulation and propaganda. He was a man who craved for power, and he knew that the best way to get it would be through mass manipulation of citizenry.

He was a guy who understood that it wasn't just about being noble and staying true to oneself. In fact, he understood that the key to amassing power was the total opposite. To gain more influence, Napoleon had to manipulate public perception. He knew that he had to portray himself as someone who the general public wanted him to be. It was through his ruthless pursuit of power wherein the *Napoleon Complex* idea comes from. Standing only 5 feet and 7 inches tall, Napoleon was considered to be rather small for a French officer.

History buffs and psychologists claim that his inferiority complex about his height made him hungrier to pursue even more power and influence.

A Tall Tale for a Short Man

Most people are going to know Napoleon as an excellent military strategist who found much success on the battlefield. However, he was more than just that. He was also a very prominent public figure who understood the importance of public perception. He knew that a person's claim to power is only as good as the amount of influence that one may have on people. He was a man who was convinced that power was fleeting and that the struggle to gain and retain it was dependent on the support of the public. He really put his principles into practice. He utilized his knowledge and understanding of propaganda to advance his interests in the political sphere of France. Until the very end of his reign, he was in the business of manipulating public opinion to favor his best interests.

This is the very reason why he still managed to suppress public denouncement and outcry despite the fact that his infantile government was at war for fourteen out of its fifteen months of existence. Napoleon was adept at establishing himself as a powerful and stable figure despite the unstable nature of the times. Napoleon made use of various political tools and machineries to advance his interests. However, what he was really good at was manipulating public opinion so that he would always have their sway.

No one can ever make the claim that Napoleon was not an ambitious man. The year is 1796, and he was practically a nobody at that time. He was just one of the many inexperienced no-name generals who were leading armies in Italian territories. But in the span of just three years, he was able to climb the ranks to become the head of the entire police force. His rise to power in such a short time was unprecedented. But it was made possible through his sheer grit and determination. Also, it helped that he was exceptionally skilled at engaging in methodical means of manipulation. He had a knack for directing and driving public opinion to better serve his interests. In July 1797, Napoleon had filed a very public complaint about French newspapers that had criticized his military tactics when he was stationed in Milan. He even went as far to say that the French papers were under the pay of the English and that they should have been broken up. Bonaparte's measures were swift and ruthless, and he was able to censor the papers from ever printing anything negative about him and his troops. He ordered his staff to make sure that newspapers were not to spread any kind of discouragement about military operations and performance so as not to lessen the morale of soldiers.

But Napoleon didn't stop at merely censoring the newspapers that were critical of him. He was also known to reign terror upon anyone that came to his way. He then decided to set up his own media platforms in an effort to boost his own public image and thwart any further efforts of negative propaganda. He recruited the help of people who were aligned with the royalist political groups–known as Club Cichy–and he established his media platforms. In just the span of one year, he was able to make six different newspaper outlets, all under his direction. These newspapers were only allowed to reflect Napoleon's own political views and make sure that he was always painted in a good light. Many of the articles that were published in these papers were even written by Bonaparte himself.

Near the end of the French revolution, in early 1799, Napoleon's army launched an invasion of Ottoman Empire-ruled Syria. The invasion campaign gained initial success, but was rather short lived as the defeat at the battle over Acre (current Israel) had shown. That summer as the Egyptian campaign was stagnating, with the political situation in France marked by uncertainty, the ever-ambitious and cunning Napoleon opted to abandon his fellow French soldiers in Egypt and return to France. Anticipating the weakened troops would likely not be of any use.

A proclamation informed the army that Bonaparte had transferred his powers as commander in chief to General called Kléber. This news was taken badly, with the soldiers angry with both Bonaparte and the French government for leaving them behind, but this aggravation soon ended, since the troops were calmed by Kléber, who convinced them that Bonaparte had not left permanently but would soon be back with reinforcements from France, which obviously was never a part of Napoleon's plans.

Dazzled by Napoleon's public campaign in the Middle East, the citizens received him with enthusiasm. However, from the moment of his return, Napoleon had already plotted a plan to take over the French's current pollical force, ultimately gaining power for himself through clever manipulation and deception over both his opponents and the French public, keeping his real intentions hidden until the end.

In November 1799, in an event known as the coup of 18 Brumaire, Napoleon was part of a group that successfully overthrew the French Directory, a committee which had governed France for the past four years during the revolution. The Directory was replaced with a new, three-member Consulate, Napoleon becoming first consul, making him France's leading political figure ending the French revolution. In June 1800, at the Battle of Marengo, Napoleon's forces defeated one of France's perennial enemies, the Austrians, and drove them out of Italy. The victory helped cement Napoleon's power as first consul.

Seeing that the country was still at mayhem from the many years of the revolution, Napoleon worked to restore stability to post-revolutionary France. He centralized the government; instituted reforms in such areas as banking and education; supported science and the arts; and sought to improve relations between his regime and the pope (who represented France's main religion, Catholicism), which had suffered during the revolution. One of his most significant accomplishments was the Napoleonic Code, which streamlined the French legal system, giving some of the basic foundation of French civil law to this day. In 1802, a constitutional amendment made Napoleon first consul for life. Two years later, he crowned himself emperor of France.

You would think that it was Napoleon's place in the army that enabled him to become such a prominent figure in France at the time. And even though he did utilize his position fairly well in his efforts to gain power, it was so much more than that. There were plenty of other charismatic officers in the military who had personalities that were just as strong. However, Napoleon always had an edge when it came to winning over the sentiment of the society as a whole. It wasn't just the military that he was working. He was also staying mindful of how the other aspects of society were perceiving him as well. True enough, establishing his own propaganda-driven newspapers helped his popularity. However, it was the publication of his own personal army reports in mainstream French publications that cemented his popularity among the French masses. He also understood that if he were to strengthen his popularity even further, he would need to gain the attention and respect of France's intellectual elite. He did so successfully with his charm and charisma. He managed to win the favor of the highest classes of France's intellectual powerhouses even prior to his Egyptian campaign. He had a roster of over 200 engineers, painters, architects, philosophers, mathematicians, and respected thinkers of various kinds under his influence. And these powerhouse thinkers had their own influence over the masses of France as well. When you pair this with the fact that Napoleon added two more newspapers to his roster of media mileage, it was starting to become clear what kind of power this man truly had. He was no longer just a soldier in the eyes of the French people. He had evolved into something much more than that. He had become a figure of the enlightenment, something divine. He was an idol. He was the outlier who they knew would never be associated with scandal, corruption, or patronage politics.

Napoleon was exceptionally skilled at writing. It was evident in the way that he constructed narratives and embedded them into his military reports. This was made even more evident whenever anyone would pit his writing against those of other generals such as Moreau. For other generals and military officers, army reports were supposed to be passive, unbiased, unemotional and dry. However, Napoleon chose to go another route with his writing, and his decision to do so served him well. Instead of just resorting to mere statements of facts and figures, Napoleon had a way of decorating his writing so that the reader felt engaged and invested. But, most importantly, it was always written in the first person to emphasize the fact that he was there and that he was making valuable contributions to the field. He was able to construct his narratives with the aid of stylish linguistics and verbiage. He played with exaggerations and hyperbole a lot to make his feats seem greater than they really were. And whenever the time came to report on negative outcomes or failed missions, he would always be quick to divert the reader's attention to success stories in an effort to distract them. Napoleon was very good at crafting his reports in a way that would enthuse and entice his readers to the point that they became invested in his personal life and dealings. While army reports were designed to be tactical narrations, Napoleon turned them into appeals to the emotions of the general public. Bonaparte's writing of his personal achievements have inspired many greater works by artists, poets, musicians, and more to add even more depth and color to the legend of Napoleon.

Given all of that, it's still important to note that Napoleon was a brilliant military strategist. No matter how hard you might try to spin it, he was an effective leader both in and out of the field. He had a mind for strategy, and he put it to good use. It wasn't just about the theatricality of his propaganda that made him so successful. He was able to build a solid foundation for his reputation by actually doing good work and showing the people that he could get the job done. All of his propaganda movements were merely supplementary to what he had already established for his own personal image. It would be unfair to brand Napoleon as a mere propaganda man who had no real depth behind his well-crafted image and public perception. He was still a person of substance. He was a formidable figure who clawed his way to the top with a little more creativity and cunning than most other people would have.

There are also other situational factors that played into Napoleon's schemes and tactics. When Napoleon had published his memoirs in 1815, he claimed that 96% of France was illiterate during his reign. This was how he justified his tough brand of leadership even though so many people had criticized him for being a dictator. However, his claims just didn't match up to the evidence of what was true at the time. It was well known that Napoleon had dedicated a lot of his time, energy, and resources into cultivating his propaganda through the press. This would not have been an effective measure if an overwhelming majority of France was illiterate at that time. The statistics indicate that in the 1680s, only around 21% of people living in France were capable of writing their own names. But by the time the 1780s came rolling around, that statistic had risen to 37%. This has led to the sentiment of multiple historians that France was largely literate by the time Napoleon had amassed his power. It might also be worth to note that Napoleon's propaganda efforts would not really have gained the traction that it did without the establishment of the political press. This was founded during the revolution that was prior to his rise to power. The establishment of the political press had further solidified proof that France was a functionally literate society and that it did not warrant the strongarm-governance that Napoleon was talking about in his memoirs. However, that did not stop him from wanting to manipulate the readers on how they perceived him and his legacy.

Another key factor and determinant that helped solidify Bonaparte's legacy was the fact that the political and democratic foundation that was set up immediately following the revolution was fairly weak. It was a system that was designed to raise the voices of the masses but, in turn, it created a vast and unmanageable division of power between the Conseil des Cinq-Cents and the Conseil des Anciens. As a result, the ensuing political conflict could not be solved through any means other than by sheer force. That's why policy-making was rarely ever civil and efficient. To add to that, the political government had very small influence over its military. It was not rare for generals to disobey orders and function under their own directives during the war. Napoleon, in particular, was guilty from this. However, due to his expert political maneuvering, he was able to exempt himself from accusations and political scrutiny. It was due to this power vacuum between the government and military wherein Napoleon saw his opportunity. There was a need for someone to be able to unite both branches, and Napoleon had a heavy footing in both. In order for the state to seek full control over France and its constituents, someone had to be able to step up to the plate. There was a need for a powerful figure who would be able to serve as the masthead for the state moving forward. It was the poor reputation of the state government and the volatility of the military that led to Napoleon's drastic rise to power.

He was able to induce nominations from members of the Directory for him to be the leader of the state. In an effort to strengthen his political campaign and claim to the seat, he used his skills in propaganda to paint the government as corrupt, inefficient, and power-hungry. He so effectively portrayed himself as the messiah who would be able to put a stop to all the nation's troubles. He was able to manipulate the public's perception of him to be one of an incorruptible hero, who they knew they could always rely on to be principled and fair.

Master of Public Perception

Despite the conclusion of the Egypt invasion, Napoleon turned it into a massive success. Even with fleeing away from Egypt, abandoning his troops, Napoleon only gained more power upon his return. By not being absent during the times of anxiety, Napoleon created distance from the issues in France, only strengthening his image in eyes of the public with his propaganda campaigns and spreading support of the French intellectuals. You can seemingly separate yourself from the everyday conflicts by simply not partaking in them. Of course, not always can you simply "disappear", but by being always available you loosen power over people as their interest on you weakens. Withdraw for a moment, keep people waiting, go work on something else, don't be available all the time and let people come to you. Manipulators know this and often utilize their accessibility to set the phase once the initial connection has been established.

He had two specific newspapers during the Egypt campaign, the "*Courrier de l'Egypte*" and the "*Décade Egyptienne*", that specifically initiated the image that Napoleon was not a mere soldier, but an enlightened leader figure, removed from the corruption of home politics and fit to cover intellectual issues. All of the publications naturally emphasized Napoleon's achievements, talking about the successes while ignoring defeats. Boldness can be used as a tool for getting people to like you even more. It relates more to the emotional side of the brain and is easier to digress. On the other hand, uncertainty and careful, scientific or rational approach is less attractive for most, because it requires more thinking and comes to us less naturally. Napoleon was great at remaining bold as well as making bold and desirable claims during uncertain times, separating himself from the crowd.

It's no secret that Napoleon's success is largely attributed to his skills as a propagandist. However, it's also important to note that the timing of his rise to power seemed to have worked to his favor as well. He was thrust into a French society that was looking for a strong powerful figure. And he knew that he had everything that he needed to meet those standards and to fit into that image as well. He was undoubtedly talented as a military official, and it was evident in his numerous achievements on the battlefield. He was an excellent writer who had the wit and charisma that could rival the great political leaders of history. People simply loved to spend time with him or hear what he had to say.

He really did have all of the tools that he needed to do what he did. It wasn't just a matter of staging a successful coup and overthrowing the people in power. He was also very skilled at keeping that power and growing it over a prolonged period of time. Napoleon had been able to bring a sense of stability to a nation that had been rocked with turmoil as a result of the revolution. He knew that being an effective leader would be nothing if the public didn't perceive him to be that way. He understood just how important it was to influence and sway public opinion to his favor by sheer will and occasional deviousness.

Whether or not Napoleon was a strong and effective leader is still a matter that is up for debate. However, what most people seem to agree on is the fact that he was an excellent propagandist who knew how to make himself look good and likable in the eyes of the people he served.

Chapter III: Machiavellian Manipulation - Lessons from The Prince

For this chapter, we aren't really going to go into detail about the real life of a particular individual. We are going to shift gears for a bit. Instead of focusing on the real-life application of manipulation, you are going to be exposed to a theoretical framework on manipulation that is focused on the sole purpose of amassing and maintaining political power. You have probably heard of the famous quote, "The end justifies the means." It's one that is uttered many times by people who are more concerned about getting results and getting things done as opposed to doing things correctly. This saying is actually attributed to one of the most influential political philosophers in history, Niccolo Machiavelli.

These days, the term "Machiavellian" is used to describe people who are devious, dishonest, and untrustworthy. It seems like people who are deemed as Machiavellian are always going to have some kind of ulterior motive that is based on an unhealthy obsession with power. However, was Machiavelli really this way? Well, not necessarily. The reason that devious people have a tendency to be associated with someone like Machiavelli is because of his most famous (probably) literary piece *The Prince*. In this timeless book, Machiavelli narrates various musings and philosophies surrounding the idea of gathering personal power. However, he doesn't really concern himself with the positive application of that power. *The Prince* is merely concerned with collecting power and making sure that one stays in power by whatever means necessary.

It's due to the ruthless nature of the principles that are touched upon in this book that Machiavelli is often illustrated as a bad example for noble and principled people.

An Enduring Machiavellian Legacy

Given the vastness and diversity of the political landscape today, it can be difficult to keep track of all the different political philosophies and pedagogies that critical groups of people might subscribe to. If you add to that the fact that many political philosophies and movements came to life and died over the course of human history, it would be hard to believe that certain political philosophies would be able to maintain relevance and influence over the course of a century. But this is something that Machiavelli was able to do with his timeless piece of work, *The Prince*. Written more than five centuries ago, the lessons, philosophies, and ethical perspectives that one might gather from

The Prince still resonate in the global political discourse today.

Machiavelli was born on the 3rd of May, 1469 in Florence, Italy. The political philosopher spent his entire professional life studying and working on various political theories and concepts. However, none of his works have endured as well and as profoundly as *The Prince* has. The main theme of the book revolves around basic rules and principles that a *prince* or a leader has to abide by to gain and retain power. Ultimately, a lot of the content of *The Prince* revolved around being ruthless, devious, and manipulative for the sole purpose of gaining power. Even for centuries after Machiavelli's death, his name became synonymous with the idea of being devious and manipulative for the sake of advancing personal interests. There is even a popular psychological test that is named after him, which looks into just how manipulative you might be as a person. You can try to search for the test online if you're ever curious about how you would fare.

A Machiavellian personality is ultimately characterized by traits of cynicism, emotional disconnect or detachment, insensitivity, and the tendency to be manipulative toward others for personal gain. At best, you would probably be able to say that the principles and methods of a Machiavellian person are morally questionable. However, there are also varying degrees to Machiavellianism as well. Typically, people who have a higher "mastery" of Machiavellian principles tend to be more strategic than they are emotionally vile. They are mostly focused on methodical behavior that would allow for them to get what they want out of life and the people that they are with.

Does the End Justify the Means?

One of the biggest principles in *The Prince* that Machiavelli placed a lot of emphasis on is the idea of having the ends justify the means. Essentially, Machiavelli claimed that as long as the desired outcome of a particular measure is achieved, then the measure in itself is justified regardless of whatever it might be. It's a very utilitarian point of view that is based on consequential moral reasoning. Based on this principle, the moral value of an act can only be measured by the consequences that follow as a result of that particular action. That is why Machiavelli argued that the employment of ruthless and vicious means to achieve a desired end is going to be justified by the effectiveness of those means. In essence, whatever you choose to do is irrelevant. It's whether you get the job done or not that matters.

So, given that that is the premise of having a Machiavellian personality type, is it really justified to be this way? Are the people who have this kind of personality type "bad" people? Well, as is always the case, morality is relative. It can be hard to determine the real morality of a person given that there are so many moral frameworks to work with. However, what Machiavellianism shows is a certain lack of empathy for other people and a lack of respect for individuality and dignity. It is also a very self-serving personality trait that seeks to always prioritize the needs of oneself even if it means trampling on the needs of other people. However, it can also be seen as a protective measure. Machiavellians can make the argument that they are only looking to protect themselves from being manipulated or exploited by other people. Whether this justification is agreeable is still up for debate.

There is a general understanding that people who carry Machiavellian traits and principles are going to be more sensitive when dealing with rejection or failure. They don't like to find themselves in positions wherein they aren't in control or they don't have a say in the outcome. They are also very goal-oriented individuals who would say or do anything to inch closer to where they want to be in life.

Is It Machiavellian to Be Strategic?

There is an argument to be had about how Machiavellianism is essentially just a demonized term for being strategic or smart. To be frank about it, someone who would be effective in employing Machiavellian principles would be someone who has a finer understanding of how people function and how the world works. It would take a great deal of insight, planning, foresight, and cognitive prowess to successfully carry out a Machiavellian game plan. That is why defenders of Machiavellian principles claim that they shouldn't really be faulted for just finding smarter ways to inch closer to their goals and dreams.

It would be hard to contest the fact that people who have a knack for strategy are going to be better at being Machiavellian. It's this kind of foresight that would allow for someone to be incredibly skilled at the manipulation of other people as a means to achieve long-term goals. Also, it's not just a matter of ruthlessness and precision either. With this manipulation, in order for it to be sustainable, Machiavellians need to make sure that they are covert so that their victims don't catch on to their methods.

Even something as simple as getting closer to someone to get them to disclose sensitive information that you might need to get ahead can be considered Machiavellian. It wouldn't be easy for just anyone to break down a person's walls and penetrate their psyche to get them to blab about a sensitive matter. However, people who have high Machiavellian levels tend to be very skilled at this.

The Key Machiavellian Principles from The Prince

Instead of deeply going into detail about the contents of *The Prince*, I am going to highlight some of its most famous passages and principles. You may find confluence with other well-known concepts as these are old but timeless principles worthy of utilizing; they apply to many parts of life. This is so you would be able to gain a more profound understanding of this philosophy. And in turn, you would be better able to identify and understand these tactics and principles in the people who you interact with daily.

Be mindful of the present.

In *The Prince*, Machiavelli stresses the importance of always staying mindful of the present. He said that in order to be an effective leader, one must always be staying on top of things. This means that a presence of mind is always going to be required in one's pursuit of power. This is largely due to the fact that in one's pursuit of power, there are bound to be various emergency situations and disasters that will require one's attention. And according to Machiavelli, a failure to stay present during those moments could possibly spell for the downfall of a leader.

He emphasizes that a true leader must be someone who is always on their toes. Naturally, the sooner that unexpected disasters are addressed, then the less damaging they would be on one's plans to gain power and success.

Be careful about who you trust.

In *The Prince*, Machiavelli is very particular about the idea of not being so liberal with trusting other people. He stresses that the pursuit of power is often a very lonely one despite the fact that you might need to use a few people or so to get to where you want to be. However, he cautions readers about the dangers of trusting people recklessly. He says that even though you might think them to be valuable allies, they might just be using you to advance their own personal agenda. He claims that while you are focused on your goals, there are many others who would be willing to be just as ruthless as you are. Always consider other people's point of view.

Read and exercise your intellect.

Machiavelli truly emphasized the value of being intelligent. He was also very adamant about how knowledge was power and how it could be used to be a protective shield against the cunning and deceitful. He stressed the importance of studying history and learning about the mistakes of the people of the past. He also encouraged readers to read more about the success stories of influential leaders and role models whom they would be able to pattern their strategies after. Machiavelli always stressed that intelligence is a key tool in one's conquests for success and achievement.

Be judicious of who you put under your employ.

Machiavelli always stressed the importance of being mindful of the people that you put under your employ to further your interests. Sure, you are going to have to resort to manipulative and devious tactics to use people to get you to where you need to be. However, this can also potentially backfire on you if you approach it in a reckless manner. You always want to make sure that you only use people who you know wouldn't serve as potential threats to your interests. Likewise, be cautious from whom you take information from.

At the end of the day, Machiavelli always stressed that you are in this alone. That means that you shouldn't really be reliant on anyone other than yourself. And for the people who you choose to include on your journey, it's very important that you know they wouldn't be doing or saying anything that would be contrary in a harming way to your principles and interests.

Learn from the greatest.

Machiavelli also stressed the importance of not always having to reinvent the wheel all of the time. As history has taught us, there have been plenty of victors in the fields of politics and business since the dawn of human civilization. According to Machiavelli, it's always important to draw as much inspiration and learning from these historical figures as much as possible. He also stressed the importance of having a mentor. Machiavelli believed that the path to greatness required substantial learning. And learning would always be more effective when it is done under the tutelage of a trustworthy mentor. Find someone who has what you want and learn from them.

Prepare for the worst.

Machiavelli emphasized the importance of preparation numerous times in his book. He always made it a point to remind the reader to have various contingency plans in place in case unexpected disasters or threats came about. Complacency is one of the biggest enemies for any follower of the Machiavellian philosophy. He went as far as to say that one should never be comfortable when they are being idle. He advised that one should always be making use of their time to fortify their defenses and sharpen their plans in preparation for the worst possible conditions. To Machiavelli, a failure to prepare was absent-mindedness, and that could prove to be costly in the pursuit of power.

Be mindful of your appearance.

This is where Machiavellian principles actually draw some similarities with Napoleon's manipulative tactics. Machiavelli stressed that it's always important for people of power to stay mindful of how they are perceived by the people around them, especially their subordinates. This resonates a lot with how Napoleon manipulated public perception to serve his own personal interests and agenda. He knew that he wouldn't be able to find success in his own dealings if he didn't have public backing. Machiavelli echoes these sentiments in The Prince as well. He said that it's very important for a leader to practice self-awareness at all times. It's not enough that a leader knows how self-righteous they are. He said that it's also just as important that other people see that they are self-righteous as well.

Almost everyone is selfish and if someone is suspiciously keen on reflecting your ideas and values or trying to prove their selflessness, it can be a sign to access more diligently. A lot of the times when we are talking it's just noise, you waiting to tell the next thing about yourself, manipulators are really good at acting like they are initially interested in your ideas to charm you, but the tricky part is judging whether someone is genuinely interested in you or not. In a conversation, do they remember what you say even after a while? Do they follow up on specific topics you've discussed in the past? How is their body language? Is the relationship balanced? It takes two to tango. It is important you are in harmony with yourself (not becoming a monk or emotionless), but being generally aware of things and reacting to emotions as rational as possible makes you a significantly harder target as often times the manipulators in fact use what you give them.

Your enemies can be your friends.

And, of course, on the matter of enemies. Machiavelli knew and understood that on the road to achievement, one would incur one's fair share of enemies along the way. This is only natural as conflict is an inevitable aspect of coexistence. This is especially true when two people are competing or vying for a coveted prize or position. However, Machiavelli stresses the importance of not totally alienating enemies just because they serve as potential threats. In fact, he turned the tables around on it. He said that enemies can also be friends in certain respects. A true Machiavellian is one who should always be able to find the value in any person they might encounter. This means that even your enemies can serve as tools or stepping stones for you to get to where you need to be in life.

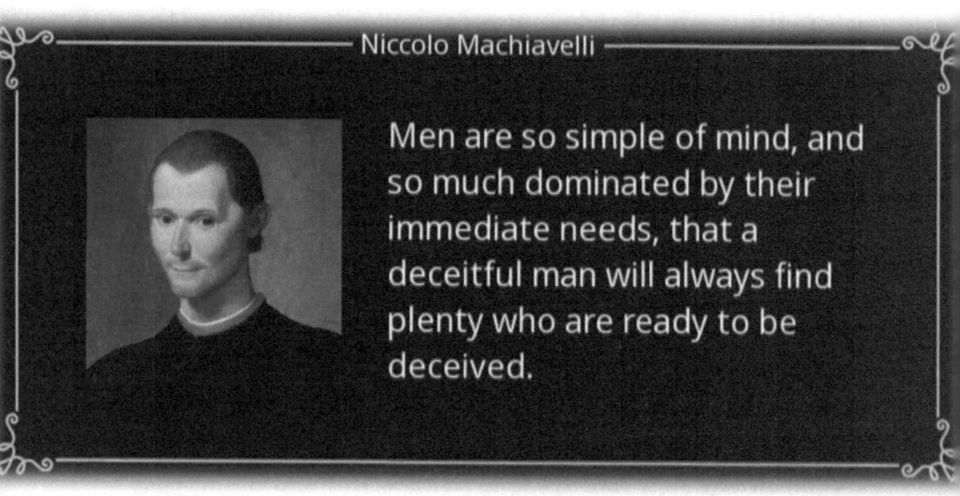

Chapter IV: Cleopatra –
Persuasive, Seductive
Manipulation

If you ask anyone on the street whether they know Cleopatra, it's likely that they would have one person's image come to mind. Cleopatra VII, even though she's the seventh of her name, is someone who many people recognize to be the only Cleopatra in history who is worth knowing. She is not just a famous historical figure. She also serves as an icon for a culture that is founded on riches, luxury, and power. Long after her death, the stories and lore of her person are still being told time and time again. Since the beginning of the civilizations, women were in fact able to become independent rulers, however, the ones who stayed on the throne the longest, had to learn specific skills to achieve it.

A lot of the time, she was portrayed as someone who was a great lover to some of the world's most powerful men. However, Cleopatra was so much more than that. She wasn't just a sex symbol. She wasn't just an icon for luxury. She was also a great student. Living in the city of Alexandria, home of a great library at the time, Cleopatra had access to the finest teachers and works of literature. She had a passion for educational endeavors since a young age, and she was largely considered to be one of the greatest minds of her time.

It's not too hard to believe that that would be the case. It's unlikely that a woman would be able to find herself in the positions that Cleopatra found herself in without possessing a certain level of intelligence. She is undoubtedly one of the strongest female figures in all of human history. Given the patriarchal nature of modern society, it would be difficult to imagine a world that is dominated by strong female personalities. However, Cleopatra was exactly that; a strong female personality who dominated the world. And she did so not just with her looks or her charm. She did so through her smarts and her intelligence, utilizing carefully crafted looks combined with her intelligence, she possessed nearly irresistible seductive skills. She didn't get to where she got by luck or accident. She made things happen.

Humble Beginnings for a Powerful Queen

Cleopatra didn't necessarily have an easy early life. She was born in 69 BC as a daughter of a pharaoh. And while her father, Ptolemy XII, was a person of influence, timing just wasn't on her side. She was born into a period of history when Egyptian culture and society were struggling to stay afloat. Her father was a great dreamer and a visionary. However, he didn't possess the skills that were necessary for him to be an effective leader and king to his people. This was a time in history when the Egyptians were completely dominated by the Romans and their thriving society. The outlook was bleak for the future of Egyptian society. The odds were not in their favor. It seemed there would no longer be powerful Egyptian rulers. But in the case of Cleopatra, she was elevated to the status of divine goddess, Isis herself, whom she publicly compared herself to, creating a whole divine aura around her. Later, she was regarded as one of the most powerful rulers in the history of Egypt and remained at the level of the pharaohs for over a decade being the last active ruler of the Ptolemaic Kingdom of Egypt.

A Queen for the Ages

It wasn't a rare occurrence for female rulers to find themselves in positions of power as a result of the death of a husband, father, or a brother. However, it was very rare for these women to make any kind of significant impact on the societies that they ruled. Usually, they would face tragic ends at the hands of adversaries or their own subjects. And they wouldn't typically be able to rule over their lands for a prolonged period of time. However, it was a completely different story for Cleopatra. She was someone who managed to elevate herself to the levels of goddesses. When she was instituted as the pharaoh of Egypt, it wasn't a quick and tragic reign for her. In fact, she reigned as Pharaoh for many years. She single-handedly changed the way that governance was carried out in Egypt, most notably with regard to foreign relations. It was her astute understanding of foreign policy that would propel her legend to even greater heights.

Her taste for power likely all started when she was just 18 years old. Her father, King Ptolemy, had made her brother, Ptolemy XIII Theos, who was just 11 years old at that time, a senior partner. However, given her seniority in age, Cleopatra took exception to this decision of her father's. She refused to acknowledge his claim to the throne, but she was still relegated to being just the junior partner due to her brother's friends in the courts.

There was a war that broke out in Rome between Pompey and Julius Caesar. Pompey had spearheaded a civil war against Caesar and had recruited the help of the younger Ptolemey and his forces. However, when Ptolemy saw that Caesar was winning the war, he decided to betray Pompey. After Pompey had lost a great battle in Greece, he then decided to flee to Egypt. It was then when Ptolemy decided to have Pompey murdered. But Caesar was not impressed with this gesture by Ptolemy, who had still been at odds with Cleopatra and her other sister, Arsinoe. Caesar had ordered for Ptolemy to step down as king and mend fences with his siblings. However, Ptolemy was not amenable to this order, and the iconic battle in Alexandria ensued where Caesar would find himself blockaded in his own palace.

This is when Cleopatra saw her opening. She decided to make her move, and she partnered with Caesar to form an alliance against her younger brother. However, this decision of Cleopatra's also cost her the loyalty of her sister. Arsione defected to Ptolemy's army to fight against the alliance of Cleopatra and Julius Caesar. During the siege of Alexandria, both Caesar and Cleopatra were able to stick things out until the arrival of Mithridates, which helped shift the battle toward their favor. Ptolemy was killed as he tried to flee the battle.

The name "Cleopatra" has become synonymous with exotic beauty and allure, but the real Cleopatra's beauty was supposedly further down the list of her charms. In fact, of her looks, Plutarch wrote, "her beauty, as we are told, was in itself neither altogether incomparable nor such as to strike those who saw her." Rather, it was the whole—her wit, her charm, and (again, according to Plutarch) "sweetness in the tones of her voice" that made her so irresistible.

Forging Political and Romantic Alliances

After the battle, Caesar paid his respects to the Ptolemaic line of leadership and had made Cleopatra's youngest brother Ptolemy the ruler of Egypt. However, it was still evident that he had been affected by her, he respected Cleopatra and her astuteness for leadership. He had made her the real power that sat behind the throne. And behind the scenes, Cleopatra and Caesar had a romantic affair, it can be said the relationship benefitted both sides. This is what led future historians to unfairly brand Cleopatra as a soulstress who merely seduced her way to the top. Whether this is an accurate description of her character is up for debate.

Cleopatra would then spend the following years conducting various missions between Egypt and Rome. As any great manipulator, she had always understood the importance of appearance. During her visits at Rome, she became a style icon for the Roman women. Her exotic yet elegant hairstyle and jewelry became a fashion trend, and according to the historian Joann Fletcher, *"so many Roman women adopted the 'Cleopatra look' that their statuary has often been mistaken for Cleopatra herself."* In a famous painting of her, we can see Cleopatra dressed in the character of Aphrodite, an ancient Greek goddess associated with love, beauty, pleasure, passion and procreation (Roman goddess Venus).

All throughout that stretch between 46 and 42 BC, she was able to maintain her authority over the courts of Egypt while making sure that the kingdom was still functional despite her absence. She understood that in order for her to strengthen the political power of her kingdom, she needed to liaise with Rome. This is when she decided to forge another political alliance with Mark Antony, the man who succeeded Caesar. However, like Cleopatra's alliance with Caesar, this bond with Antony was more than just a political one. There were romantic components to it as well. Anthony was a man who loved pleasure, excitement and fancy leisure. Cleopatra understood her victim's desires and intentionally showed him the superiority of the most spectacular Egyptian parties, winning Anthony's support. It was because of this alliance that she was able to cement herself as Rome's primary ally throughout this epoch. She was able to secure Egypt's independence, sovereignty, and geographical advantage as a result of this partnership that she had formed with Antony.

Another fruit of this alliance was Antony's ordered assassination of Arsinoe at Ephesus. Cleopatra and Mark Antony would later wed despite the fact that Antony was already married to Octavian's sister. This marriage between Antony and Cleopatra would alienate a lot of affected parties and would sever ties between various Roman allies.

Ultimately, Cleopatra had spent the rest of her reign dabbling into Roman politics. She is well-remembered for her role in helping Antony fight against Octavian during the second Triumvirate War. However, her decision to stay at Antony's side would also prove to be her own undoing. When Cleopatra saw the impending defeat of Antony's army, she decided to commit suicide in an effort to save herself from the same and the torture of being imprisoned.

Chapter V: Combatting Manipulation

Fighting off manipulative tactics and advances is more than just being able to identify it. Sure, it helps to know that you are being manipulated whenever that truly is the case. That means that you aren't being naive about your situation. However, it's also just as important that you are able to know the common tactics in dealing with cunning or not so cunning people who seek to manipulate you for their own personal gain. That is exactly what this chapter is going to orient you with.

You've already been exposed to the many faces of manipulation and the kind of impact that it can have on not just one, but on a large group of people. Now, you have to learn how you would be able to spot manipulative behavior in your everyday life. And in addition to that, you have to know how you're going to deal with it whenever you find yourself in those situations as well. It's not very rare for people to find themselves in manipulative situations and not know what to do about it. This is not by accident. Manipulative people have a way of compromising their victims' inhibitions and better judgment. That's why a lot of victims of manipulation can often feel paralyzed by the situations that they find themselves in.

What this chapter seeks to do is offer these types of people a way out. You don't always have to be a victim of your circumstances. If you know that you are in danger of being manipulated, then you need to do something about it. The will to act is entirely up to you. This chapter is going to provide you with the proper know-how to help you get yourself out of whatever bind you might be in.

How to Spot Manipulative Behavior

Spotting manipulative behavior in another person isn't always going to be an easy feat. After all, the best manipulators are those who know how to hide their intentions quite well. It might seem like you're just getting chummy with someone and that there isn't any malice behind it. However, with the master manipulators, there are a lot of things that are going on behind the scenes that you might not even be aware of. It can become particularly difficult to identify manipulative behavior when you don't make an active effort to try to seek it out.

Of course, you always want to be maintaining an optimistic and positive view of the world. If you are someone who just generally has a positive disposition, no one should have the right to tell you to be any other way. That is your own prerogative. However, just because you want to stay positive doesn't mean that you should be naive and reckless with the people you let into your life. You are still going to want to stay guarded to a certain degree. Even though you might put yourself at the risk of sounding snobby or unapproachable, that's just the trade-off that you're going to have to make to protect yourself.

The key to picking clues from people is learning to become a student of deep listening and observing. This however, is pointless unless you can actually maintain a form of interest in what the person is saying. Make it appear natural. Don't let them realize you are analyzing them. You have to be interested or at least intensely focused on what they are giving away.

One may argue, everywhere we go people, circumstances, and forces beyond our control manipulate us in a certain way. And while there often are manipulative tricks being used, focusing or being paranoid about every last little incident being "manipulation" is rather pointless as well. First and foremost, we want to focus our efforts on the most tangible occasions that may be of direct harm, being rational on when to assess manipulative behavior is the key. Hence just a single red flag every now and then is only natural for us humans. If you notice a lot of these signs might actually be present in a relationship that you have with someone in your life, then you might want to step back a little to reflect deeply on your own. It's possible that this human being is manipulating you.

Look out for cues, any recurring traits of manipulation to occur in the future.

The relationship makes you feel scared

Here's a general tip: if a relationship is built entirely out of a foundation of fear, then you know that it might not be a good one to be in. It's normal to feel intimidated or even somewhat fearful of certain people. Perhaps, you might be meeting someone you admire and idolize. To feel somewhat intimidated by that individual is okay to a certain degree. However, when you start building a close and intimate relationship with the person and the fear still doesn't go away, then that is definitely a bad sign.

Manipulators understand fear very well, and they know how to use it against those who don't have good control over their phobias. For instance, say you've been planning something for a while and the person always comes up with last-minute changes that give them what they want, they are utilizing your fear of losing something. In this case the time and emotional attachment spent making and almost executing the plan. They will utilize the fear that you have of them into making you do things that would benefit them even if it means compromising your own well-being. This is why you should always be wary of relationship environments that reek of fear and intimidation.

You are made to feel guilty about everything you do

Somehow, you are made to feel guilty about everything that you do. When you are in a manipulative relationship, nothing that you ever do is going to be right or correct. Even when you have the best intentions and you are sure about your execution, there's still always something for you to feel bad about. Generally, a manipulative individual is going to avoid making you feel validated for your efforts or your actions. This is because they want you to feel like you need to work harder to be worthy of their attention and approval.

This is a tactic that is designed to bully a person into thinking that they're not doing enough so that they feel pressured to become better. It's a kind of negative reinforcement that is quite common in a lot of abusive relationships all over the world. It's the same way a boss would tell a worker that their work is mediocre to get that worker to keep on trying harder out of guilt or shame.

You often question your own beliefs

Gaslighting is another common technique that is usually employed by manipulative individuals with the purposes of distorting an individual's view of reality. As a victim, you are made to doubt your own beliefs and perspectives on things so that you grow reliant and dependent on another person. Essentially, you are made to distrust your own senses and instincts so that you will be forced to cling onto someone else to help you stay grounded and sane.

Manipulative individuals are so good at distorting the facts and stretching the truth to the point that they make lies seem believable even when they're completely outrageous. In essence, they are just thrusting their own version of "reality" down your throat.

You are made to feel like there are always strings

attached

Nothing you ever do in this kind of relationship is going to come without any strings attached. You just get the sense that if you are going to be on the receiving end of some nice treatment, it's never something that you can just take at face value. You notice that there's a pattern that's emerging here whenever this person does anything that adds value to your life. You always just come to expect that there are going to be some kind of ulterior motives behind it. You would just find it very difficult to just take a compliment or be on the receiving end of a kind gesture. You somehow get the sense that that isn't the whole story.

Your insecurities are always thrust into the limelight

One of the grandest ways in which a manipulative person would get you to become emotionally vulnerable would be to highlight your insecurities. Naturally, as a human being, you have your fair share of insecurities. We all do. And the manipulative individual knows this more than anyone. However, instead of being sensitive and empathetic toward these insecurities that you might have, they use it as ammo. They are going to capitalize on these insecurities to make you feel terrible about yourself, setting the brain into more reactive, survival mode.

In psychology, whenever an individual engages in self-hatred or self-loathing, they find a strong power figure with whom they can cling onto. The manipulative master knows this, and that's how they will want to present themselves in your life. They will make it seem like you need them to be there for you because of how incompetent you end up perceiving yourself to be. When you're with a manipulative person, you will constantly be bombarded with reminders of your personal vulnerabilities. Spark insecurities or question people's identity to create "issues" people didn't know they had and then allay these insecurities offering the solution, also commonly used in marketing.

Complex art of spotting manipulation

In case of the manipulator being more sophisticated one, it may be tricky to combat their charms and craftiness. When the goal is to manipulate a person without them ever catching you, to get them to do what you want, the key is letting people think it's their own free will to make a decision.

Orchestrate a setup for people to want to help your case. Nobody likes when someone is trying to change their opinion. Would you like simply being told to try out smoking if you were not a smoker? However, ask a regular smoker why they smoke and you might get an answer such as "I can't go without", in this case the dopamine receptors release a small dose of gratification each time the person has a cigarette, the same can be applied to all addictions or self-sabotaging acts. People are more likely to help one's case if they feel involved, or there's something for them to gain.

In marketing, sell the brand. You don't want to tell people to buy your item but to sell it to them. Make them feel like they can't go without and you are the solution. Get to know your target's weaknesses and soften people's resistance by confirming their self-opinion. Phony confessions usually receive an honest one in return, this one can be rather difficult to assess, but if you can catch a faked confession it is usually a sign of extremely sophisticated and cold-blooded manipulator.

In such a case of facing a sophisticated, individual manipulator, look for secrets or holes in their past they have tried to keep hidden. If you know the individual personally, you can recall back at occurrences where they felt great insecurity, aggression or defensive behavior over seemingly tiny matter. You can try to scare them off if you can find leverage that threatens their control.

Again, if at all possible, the easiest choice would be to cut this individual out of your life immediately. Manipulative people have strong tendency for controlling everything around them. For instance, aggressive type manipulators often show physical aggression over small details such as always walking ahead of people, taking over as much space as they possibly can needing to be in control at all times. Do something completely unexpected and watch carefully how they react, the more sudden and stressful the situation, the better. The key to picking clues from people is learning to become a student of deep listening and observation. This however, is pointless unless you can actually maintain a form of interest in what the person is saying. Make it appear natural. Don't let them realize you are analyzing them. You have to be interested or at least intensely focused on what they are giving away.

You feel a lot of pressure to be a certain way

And, of course, you know that something is wrong whenever you are constantly pressured to be a certain way. No functional relationship should spare any room for unwarranted pressure on an individual. If you have people in your life who have certain expectations of you, then that should be fine. However, be very wary of those people who seemingly place you on a pedestal. They might be hyping you up to your face just to see how much they would be able to get out of you. They would make you feel as if it would be a complete tragedy for you to disappoint them by not delivering. Affirmation is also a powerful manipulation tool. Repeating a simple message subtly over time gets plant into people's subconscious permanently without them even realizing it. Think of any marketing slogans that come to mind.

How to Deal with a Manipulative Person

Psychological manipulation is always going to be a very loaded and heavy-handed issue. It can often be referred to as lying, deceiving, skewing, distorting, gaslighting, intimidating, guilting, and other such things. Manipulators can also take the form of many different people over the course of your life. Sometimes, the person who is manipulating you might be a parent, sibling, boss, classmate, coworker or romantic partner, among others. That's why manipulation is such a complex topic to handle. It can take the form of various tactics, and it can also be employed by various agents. This is why it can be increasingly difficult for someone to be able to identify and deal with a manipulative person.

In the earlier parts of this chapter, you were briefed on what a manipulative relationship might look like. You were exposed to the many different feelings, sensations, and experiences that you might have should you ever find yourself in a manipulative relationship environment. As long as you keep your eyes peeled and you make an active effort in seeking these red flags out, it shouldn't really be a problem. Now, it's a matter of dealing with these people and managing their advances.

First evaluate whether the person is more of a systematic or unconscious manipulator. The more systematic, profound manipulators are almost certainly beyond reach. They can have grand visions and don't care who they have to get by to pursue their goals, they may simply enjoy controlling others, perhaps they have had childhood traumas and issues that lead them to exploit others for fulfillment. These types of people are more aware of it and aggressively pursue their manipulative traits.

Whatever the case may be, if possible, keep your distance on these types of people. Indeed, the easy solution would be to cut this person out of your life, right? It can be so easy to just burn bridges with someone if you know that they have manipulative tendencies and that they would be so willing to advance their own personal interests at your expense. That kind of selfishness should warrant a cutting of ties.

However, it's not always going to be that simple. There are going to be times when the person who is manipulating you is someone you have a deep bond and connection with. There is even a chance they are not consciously aware of their behavior themselves. For instance, if your parent, partner or friend is manipulating you, it's not going to be so easy to just break that relationship off entirely. This is especially true if you love your parents and you know that they love you in return. In this case, it's not just a matter of eliminating a manipulative person from your life.

Rather, it becomes an issue of managing this individual.

When dealing with a manipulative person, it's very important that you tread lightly. Keep in mind that there is also a paternal kind of manipulation. They might not have bad intentions, and they might take offense to the fact that you are accusing them of being manipulative. That is why you have to be extra cautious and sensitive when you broach the issue with them. This segment of the chapter is going to guide you all throughout this meticulous process because it really is an intensive one especially if you're not looking to completely alienate this individual from your life.

First, Be Safe

If you know that you are in danger whenever you are with this manipulative individual in your life, always make sure that there is a third-party present. You can never really know what they might do to you if the two of you are alone. So, before you confront them about your manipulation, make sure that you have someone else in the room. You need that mediator; someone who would be able to help bridge the two of you. You can always call on a mutual friend, a shared loved one, or a trusted confidante. In more serious cases, you can even seek professional help from a licensed therapist. The point here is that the confrontation process should never be conducted recklessly. Your safety is always going to be the first priority here. And a lot of the time, that means having someone else in the room to be with you.

Take a Diplomatic Approach to Initiating a Dialogue

You can either choose to work your own influence on them to lessen the negative effects, or you could just confront them. The initial confrontation doesn't have to be so hot and impassioned. In fact, the best approach to confronting this individual would be to be as calm and collected as can be. You want to make sure that you are taking emotions out of the equation here. Keep in mind that a manipulative person is always going to capitalize on the emotionality of a person. If you take that ammo away from them, then it leaves them very little to work with. In addition to that, it's more likely that they won't react in such a hostile manner if you take a more civil approach to initiating this dialogue with them. Using people's own words against them makes it harder to resist whatever it is you are asking them to do, if one claims to be selfless, then they would not partake in certain actions to begin with.

You have to remember that starting the conversation isn't always going to go so smoothly. It's very much likely that they will resist at first. However, you need to stay persistent. You have to emphasize the importance of this conversation. If they still show an unwillingness to engage in this kind of dialogue, then skip to the last phase of this subchapter. However, if they do decide to engage with you in this conversation, then you need to stay mindful of the following tips.

Don't Fight Back

If they are going to be hostile with you about it, resist the urge to fight back. You have to learn to pick your spots. Responding to them in a hostile manner is only going to result in you playing into their games. You don't want that. You want to make sure that you stay calm all throughout. When they get emotional, don't invalidate these feelings. Their emotions might actually be very authentic regardless of whether they are based on distorted truths or not. A person can still feel angry about something that is a complete lie or fantasy. Keep that in mind.

Instead of invalidating their feelings and telling them that they're being unreasonable, hear them out. With this method, you will get a chance to really understand them more. You will be able to gain insight into their behavioral triggers. The more you understand them, then the better it will be for you to manage this entire situation.

Set Clear Limits and Boundaries

Once you have heard their side of the tale, it's now time for you to air out your personal grievances. Again, you need to make sure that you keep emotions out of it. You don't want them to be invalidating what you're saying just because you're being hysterical. You want to be honest about it, and be straight. You shouldn't be beating around the bush anymore. Make sure that all of the skeletons come out of the closet. Be courteous, but also, don't pull any punches. No matter how uncomfortable it might be to speak honestly about your feelings, you're going to have to do so.

If you're interested in salvaging the relationship, then emphasize this point. Make sure they understand that you don't want to block them out of your life completely. However, you also need to emphasize that you will be setting clear limits and boundaries as you move forward in your relationship together. Make them understand that the integrity of your relationship is dependent on their respect for the boundaries that you set in it.

Know When It's Time to Walk Away

Sometimes, you just need to be able to know when it's time to walk away. No matter how painful it is to cut yourself loose from someone who you love dearly, you still have to do so for the sake of your own well-being. You should not be making any room for toxicity or manipulative behavior that causes burden in your life regardless of who it might be coming from. At the end of the day, the only real person who has your back is yourself. That is why you have to make it a point to protect yourself at all costs. If there is no way for you to find a peaceful means of coexisting with one another that doesn't involve any form of harmful manipulation that is taking value out of your life, then you need to be able to walk away from that.

Granted, walking away from someone who is close to you isn't going to be a quick and easy process. It's going to be a very painful and gradual one. However, you always need to prioritize your own well-being above the relationships that you have with others, especially if they are the toxic and systematic type. Stay safe and guarded. No relationship is worth losing your sense of self over.

Epilogue

Hopefully, you will have picked something up from this book that could add value to your life and the lives of those around you. Again, it's important to emphasize that this book has no agenda other than to provide insight and understanding into how manipulative behavior works. Being a citizen of this planet, you owe it to yourself and to the people around you to be a well-functioning individual. This has long been established in an unwritten social contract that has evolved over the course of generations.

Like Niccolo Machiavelli put it: *"a deceitful man will always find plenty who are ready to be deceived"*.

This is precisely why it's important for you to develop a fundamental understanding of manipulative behavior and maintaining a level of respect for a person's dignity and autonomy. Coexistence is key when it comes to preserving the integrity and the very fabric of society. It would be contradictory to the principles of coexistence to allow a culture of manipulation and deceit to flourish out of proportion. As has been evidenced by the case studies that were covered in this book, manipulation doesn't necessarily try to promote the common good of everyone. In fact, in a lot of cases, only the interests of a select few (and in the most extreme cases, just one person) are prioritized at the expense of the many. Even if the initial idea may be good, the greed takes over.

Earlier in this book, we touched upon how manipulation is a violation of a person's individuality. And as you were gradually exposed to various cases of mass manipulation such as Napoleon during the French revolution or the Ponzi's scheme, you might have gained further insight into how destructive and dangerous manipulative behavior can be, even if it starts out noble. Engaging in manipulative behavior is considered to be an affront to the dignity of a human being. Everyone, however, is free to make their choice. It's no secret that modern society is composed of various classes and groupings. What manipulation does is that it allows for the privileged and powerful to wreak further havoc on the lives of the underprivileged and downtrodden. In that sense, there is no proper balance of power which further indicates an unhealthy base level of dysfunction within our society that has always been present in the history of human societies, merely manifesting itself in different forms. The idea of manipulation as a tool for people to get ahead at the expense of the weak and vulnerable is not something new, it is as old as man-mane systems.

Regardless of your genuine intensions for seeking to understand manipulation, this book is a contribution to the effort to tip the scales a little. People in power are in more convenient positions to actually engage in manipulative behavior against the weak, less educated.

However, it takes two to tango. And as we saw from the examples, one may argue a form of manipulation is necessary for one to advance their perceived ranking in the society. Most importantly, manipulative advances and tactics can be thwarted as long as victims are able to arm themselves properly. Consider this book to be an addition to that arms race. Outfox the Fox. I hope this book gave you some ideas or insights on different occasions where you may have been fooled. All of us have experienced different levels of manipulation for the sake of advancing other peoples' interests, and even if you haven't, you'll likely find yourself facing situations at some point in your life where understanding manipulation proves helpful. In order to defend yourself against the enemy, you first have to understand what you're dealing with.

Understanding manipulation is no easy feat. And this book alone might not necessarily be enough to equip you with all of the knowledge that you need to know. However, every gradual process requires a starting point. And if you are only beginning your journey toward understanding manipulation and how you can better protect yourself from its treachery, then hopefully, this book will have been able to help you out. Granted, with such a diligent topic there are always going to be certain variables that can only be learned through deliberate thinking, time and effort.

At the very least, you should already be equipped with a foundational skills to ensure that you don't allow yourself to become a victim of manipulation so easily.

As a living and breathing human being, you owe it to yourself to always uphold your sense of dignity and individuality. You never want to allow anyone in your life, regardless of the nature of the relationship that you have with them, to ever manipulate you for their own best interests. Despite the dark subject, accepting that manipulation exists all around us doesn't mean that you can't be spreading light and positive influence to the world. Simply be aware of it.

Machiavelli might have argued that the ends always justifies the means. However, in this scenario, no ends are ever going to be able to justify you losing a sense of ownership over your own life. May this book serve as a tool for you to always defend your individuality and your dignity. You should never be put in a position wherein you have to compromise either of those things. The very essence of human agency at the current day and age is built on the idea that you are your own person with inalienable rights and freedom. If both of those things are threatened by manipulative advances, then you owe it to yourself to defend them.

This has been Outfox the Fox, Understanding Manipulation. If you found the contents of this material useful, feel free to share it with others that may benefit of it.

Bibliography

Clark, D. (2018, January 13). Cleopatra: Egyptian Seductress or Savvy Politician. Retrieved from http://semiramis-speaks.com/cleopatra-egyptian-seductress-or-savvy-politician/

https://www.history.com /ancient-history/cleopatra

Duncan, J. (2019, August 20). Why Manipulative People Manipulate Us: The Child Within Them and How to Deal With Them. Retrieved from https://medium.com/moments-of-passion/why-manipulative-people-manipulate-us-the-child-within-and-how-to-deal-with-them-2d5966c0c400

Fisher, T. (2004, April 27). The Napoleonic Wars: The Rise and Fall of an Empire

Gander, K. (2019, May 6). 550 years since Niccolo Machiavelli was born-how to check how Machiavellian you are. Retrieved from https://www.newsweek.com/550-years-niccolo-machiavelli-was-born-how-check-how-machiavellian-you-are-1408155

Greene, R. (2003). *The Art of Seduction*

Horn, J. (2015, July 17). What Made Napoleon a Great Leader? Retrieved from http://discerninghistory.com/2015/07/what-made-napoleon-a-great-leader/

Klimczak, N. (2016, July 14). The Wisdom of Cleopatra, the Intellectual Queen Who Could Outsmart Them All. Retrieved from https://www.ancient-origins.net/history-famous-people/wisdom-cleopatra-intellectual-queen-who-could-outsmart-them-all-006280

Machiavelli, N. (1952). *The prince*. New York, NY: The New American Library.

(n.d.). Nature and History of Ponzi Schemes. Retrieved from http://www.sjsu.edu/faculty/watkins/ponzi.htm

Noggle, R. (2018, March 30). The Ethics of Manipulation. Retrieved from https://plato.stanford.edu/entries/ethics-manipulation/

Shortsleeve, C. (n.d.). How to Tell If Someone Is Manipulating You-And What to Do. Retrieved from https://time.com/5411624/how-to-tell-if-being-manipulated/

Soeiro, L. (2018, July 25). 4 Ways to Deal With Manipulative People. Retrieved from https://www.psychologytoday.com/intl/blog/i-hear-you/201807/4-ways-deal-manipulative-people

Valentin. (2013, October 12). How important was Napoleon Bonaparte's use of propaganda and censorship in the rise and consolidation of his power in France? (Part 1, by Valentin Boulan). Retrieved from https://publishistory.wordpress.com/2013/07/31/how-important-was-napoleon-bonapartes-use-of-propaganda-and-censorship-in-the-rise-and-consolidation-of-his-power-in-france-part-1/

www.ingramcontent.com/pod-product-compliance
Lightning Source LLC
Chambersburg PA
CBHW031141250726

48655CB00002B/787